Who was Jesus of Nazareth?
His Childhood and Youth

Who was Jesus of Nazareth?

His Childhood and Youth

Followers of Jesus of Nazareth

The WORD
The UNIVERSAL SPIRIT

1st Edition – March 2013

Published by:
© Universal Life
The Inner Religion
P.O. Box 3549
Woodbridge, CT 06525
U S A

Licensed edition
translated from the original German title:
"Wer war Jesus von Nazareth?
Seine Kindheit und Jugendjahre"
with the consent of
© Gabriele-Verlag Das Wort GmbH
Max-Braun-Str. 2, 97828 Marktheidenfeld
Germany

Order No. S 170ENPOD
The German edition is the work of reference for all
questions regarding the meaning of the content.

All rights reserved

ISBN: 978-1-890841-71-3

Preface

Over and over again, people from all over the world ask us to report about the true life of Jesus of Nazareth. Many people are disappointed by the churches and are fed up with hearing over and over again, especially on church holidays, the same old discourses from the churchmen, who cannot give any answers to the questions about life.

In this book, followers of the Nazarene will give an authentic report on the life of Jesus of Nazareth, free of the interpretations of the caste of priests and of the falsifications of historians servile to the church and such who, commissioned by the churches, wrote, and still write, the history books.

More and more people are seeking the true Jesus of Nazareth, the Christ of God, and cannot find Him in the churches of stone. As mentioned above, they are fed up with not getting from the priestmen of the institutional churches any answers to the questions about life, which would find an echo in their seeking soul and would mean a gain for their own life. Are you also one of the many people, who, year after year, above all, at the so-called Christian celebrations of the churches, submit yourself again and again to the same old story about Jesus of Nazareth from the viewpoint of the caste of priests? Year in and year out, over and over again, the same dogmatic ceremonies, rites and cults. Year in and year out, over and over again, the same meaningless liturgies, the hollow and unctuous sermons from priests, bishops and cardinals, including the pope. Often, they even preach to the unsuspecting folk the exact opposite of the supposedly infallible proclamations of doctrine and dogmas of their own church, thus freely leading the lemmings

– according to church doctrine – straight into "eternal damnation," according to the motto: The common folk won't notice any way. Year in and year out, no real answers from the priestmen to the questions about the deeper meaning of life and the "why" in regard to the events in everyday life.

At best, they try to convince a seeking person of the alleged mysteries of God. And with this, the ecclesiastical wisdom of the priests, including the pope, has come to an end, since, allegedly, faith is enough, even though Jesus of Nazareth said something totally differently. Honestly speaking, most of us are, in truth, fed up with the fact that year after year, the risen Christ of God is repeatedly mocked and scorned anew by the institutional church leaders of this world. Shouldn't it finally come to an end, that He, Jesus, the Christ, who, as stated, is the resurrected Christ of God, the Co-

Regent of the heavens, is presented over and over again to the incense-clouded people as the Jesus of Nazareth who was defeated by the caste of priests and as the tortured, lifeless trophy nailed to the cross?

Every person should be allowed to live according to his faith, as he wants to. Anyone can belong to a religion, as he wants to. But when Jesus, the Christ, whom the so-called Christian churches invoke, is slandered, discriminated against, and His life as well as His teachings is turned into the exact opposite, beyond all measure, continuously, and in the worst way, then followers of the Nazarene will not remain silent about this and will repeatedly point out the abuse of His name.

Many fellow people may be wondering why so many questions, requests and feedback are directed to the followers of Jesus of Nazareth. There are simply many people to whom the truth is important. This is why they want followers of the Nazarene to report about the life of Jesus, the Christ. Very many people in almost all the countries and on all the continents of the Earth know that more than 36 years ago, God, the Eternal, the God of Abraham, Isaac and Jacob, the God of all true prophets, again called a person to be His prophetess. It is Gabriele, whom God, the Eternal, calls His emissary and prophetess, and through whom the Spirit of the Christ of God has given thousands of public revelations and spiritual schoolings to mankind. She is truly the last prophet in a great cycle, a great teaching prophet, whom God, the Eternal, sent to mankind before the turn of time will change many things, and Jesus, the Christ of God, appears in Spirit.

Followers of Jesus of Nazareth

𝒢od's infinite wisdom revealed to mankind through His prophetess, Gabriele, what was already announced by Jesus of Nazareth, who promised 2000 years ago: *"I will send you the Comforter, who will guide you into all the truth."*

The Comforter is the Christ of God, who, in the prophetic word through His instrument for the present time, through the prophetess of God, has revealed to mankind the truth of the heavens for all spheres of life, insofar as people can understand it.

From several revelations by the Christ of God through His prophetess, Gabriele, various excerpts have been compiled here, which describe the life on Earth of Jesus of Nazareth in His own words of revelation.
Who was Jesus of Nazareth?

In the great Christ-revelation *»This Is My Word – Alpha and Omega. The Christ-revelation which true Christians the world over have come to know«*, Christ reveals the following:

"The Comforter is the Spirit of Christ, who I Am, the life in God, My Father. The Spirit of the Christ of God is omnipresent in the four natures of God, the powers of drawing and of creating – which every soul bears in itself as power and life. The Comforter, My Spirit, is the Redeemer-spark, in which comfort and redemption are active. The redemption is My work, which I received from the Father for the home bringing of all souls and men."

And Christ revealed further:

"The Spirit of truth is the Christ of God of whom I, as the Son of Man, spoke. I fulfilled these promises during these almost two thousand years. The Spirit of truth came in all generations, and His work in this world increased in light and power more and more, for many people heard and read about the law of life, the eternal truth, and many a person began to develop the life within himself.

Nevertheless, in this turn of time, the light – I, the Christ, the eternal truth – breaks through in a broad spectrum and radiates into the whole world. The law of truth flows through the prophetic word as a wide stream; for I sent the divine wisdom to the people, so that the truth may be revealed and shake up the people who live in the constraints of the world and in sin. The truth also reveals what is in the present and what will come. It gives to drink and re-

freshes many souls and people and strengthens them with love, power and wisdom. The one who clears up his sins will recognize Me, the Christ, for sin clouds the spiritual eye. The one who is able to see recognizes Me, the Christ, in himself and in those who truly follow Me ... As the Son of Man, I left the people. As the Christ of God, their Redeemer, the Spirit of truth, I Am come again."

Thus far, a short excerpt from the great Christ-revelation »*This Is My Word – Alpha and Omega*«.

The high Spirit of the Christ of God, also revealed to us through Gabriele, the prophetess and emissary of God, a segment of His life on Earth as the child of Mary and Joseph. And so, He, Himself, the Christ of God, revealed to us from His own life on Earth; and we want to quote several passages from these words of revelation, to also rehabilitate Him, Jesus, the Christ:

"My life as the boy Jesus was marked by poverty. This, too, was a symbol for mankind, for the Lord said: 'I am especially to be found with the poor and those in need of help. The High-ran King and the rich are an abomination to Me.' God, in His greatness, is modest. He proved this in the earthly garment of Jesus. He, God in Me, in a poor boy, often beset by need and physical privation.

As a child, I wanted to be among other children. But since Mary was not welcome among the Nazarene people – and thus, nor Jesus – they regarded us with hostility. The playmates to which I then turned were not the children of Nazareth, but the animals. I spent many hours in nature, so as to talk with My friend – a beetle or another animal. In My heart, I heard the answer of the animals. I felt secure among them. Through Mary, My mother on

Earth, and through the answer of the animal world, the Spirit of God led Me on the path to God consciousness.

I experienced the tied-up animals, as well as the living beings in the fields and in the gardens that surrounded the humble cottage in Nazareth."

The boy Jesus asked many, many questions of His mother, Mary. Jesus, the Christ, Himself, revealed more about this to us:

"Maria could not answer all the questions for me, but she said: 'My son, many people live in the bondage of their disbelief. A person who is not free in his heart has little understanding for the animals. The Lord, who dwells in your heart, can give you better information on this than I, His humble handmaid.'

The Lord in Me began to stir only when Mary called my attention to this over and over again.

'Mother,' so came the next question from Jesus, 'Why did Moses hear God and why do you hear Him? – I know that when you are sitting quietly on the bench before our cottage, you are in a dialogue with God, our Father.' ...
Now Mary began: 'My son, it is high time that you immerse yourself in the truth, for God, our Father, has been speaking to you for a long time. The sensations of the animals that You hear within You are also the voice of the Lord, for nothing lives outside of Him.'
It was Mary who led Me to the inner voice, and when I heard it, it made me happy as nothing before, which says: My voice is soft and sweeter than honey.

The boy Jesus was brought up in the name of the Lord and according to His will. He was raised very simply. Joseph, a high spirit being from the homeland, as well as Mary, were both clad in a poor human body ... They lived among the poor; their language was simple, as was their standing. I spoke the same language as did My foster parents and all the poor among the people. Only My soul was vivified by the divine breath and raised to be loving and merciful.

I shared my childhood experiences with My parents, but they had little understanding for them, because they did not know how to interpret these strange experiences and, therefore, could not comprehend them."

The resurrected Jesus, the Christ of God, Himself, continued to reveal about His youth: *"When I grew older and My soul passed from childhood into adolescence, God revealed Himself in more visions ... Through this, My soul was trained in love and mercy. Even as a child, I had spiritual powers that I some-*

times applied wrongly, and from which I, Jesus, could also learn.

The law says: Every human being and every soul will be led by way of their own mistakes and weaknesses, until they recognize them and work on themselves.

Jesus was not spared anything. He had to live and learn just like any other person. And so, from childhood on, I had to recognize My human weaknesses and learn to overcome them, because I was a symbol for mankind. My soul was trained by the Spirit of the Father ... My external life was calm, but My inner life was all the stormier. Day and night, I had visions; they often presented Me with human difficulties ... What I could not interpret during this time, I gave to My Father with the plea: 'When My soul has matured, O Lord, surely You will reveal this vision to Me again.' All visions became ever clearer to Me during the course of My years as apprentice and journeyman ...

Whoever wants to achieve a victory over the base forces must first declare war on the tempter. For without a fight against the adversary there is no victory over the insidious, base nature that in the three-dimensional world insinuates itself and gains dominion over the sensory world of the people ...

The boy Jesus entered adolescence, a storm and stress period, which often kept Him away from his parents' house for many days. Joseph was sometimes annoyed; Mary was anxious, and then without understanding. Jesus became uncommunicative and went His own way.

When I stayed away from My work for several days, I made it up afterwards. God, My Father, gave Me the strength to quickly make up all the carpenter work I had failed to do during the days I stayed away.

The people who Joseph worked for knew about the powers of Jesus and therefore took a shine to Me. Often, Joseph would get a job only if he assured them that Jesus would also be on the job. And I did this, to please the aging father Joseph, because My taciturn ways, My reticence as well as My frequent absences, often made Joseph quite annoyed.

My heart was heavy during My work, because I came to know the people. They were very worried about their external possessions, less, however, about the salvation of their soul. They were citizens of Nazareth, who did not love Me with their heart. They respected Me only as a carpenter, because I did good and fast work. But they were the same ones who talked badly about Jesus on the Sabbath, because I did not go with them to the synagogue or temple.

As a child I would walk at Mary's hand to the temple every now and then. And when I was a child of approximately 12 years, I visited the temple servants. But the free person, Jesus, avoided the mostly fraudulent "divine" spells that spilled into rites and the like.

I heard the Father in My heart and knew that He was not external, but a God of the inner eternal kingdom. And I spoke of this in the temple when I was twelve, whereupon the scribes jeered and ridiculed Me. ...

It is written in the scriptures: The intellectual person rarely understands a person of the heart. But God is the heart. A person who does not have the sensation of the heart remains in the intellect, and his deed will be accordingly ...

Much has already been written about the boy Jesus, but much remained hidden: The unspeakable grief in a person whose soul showed him everything, but to whom words are lacking to express what he experienced. I set forth all the sensations of My soul in the many parables.

As a child and a young man, I had unimaginable complexes. The intelligence of God was My sensation. Because of this, I was far superior to other people ... but I could only put into writing the most necessary things. I struggled with these complexes ... Again and again, I was exposed to the ridicule of the Pharisees and scribes ...

Many words have been said about My life as Jesus. Here, the Christ, does not want to reveal in word more than is necessary. What I am explaining here was and is a symbol for mankind.

My heart is sad, and the burden of the cross lies on my spiritual shoulders and in the unbelieving souls and people. ...

After a life of wrestling with the forces of darkness day and night, My preaching ministry began. The darkness wanted to stop the development of the Son of God. With all the powers available to them, they fell upon Me day and night, to prevent the completion of redemption.

The hardest years of My life on Earth, of which the world knows little, were the years between the age of 12 and the years of My preaching. They brought Me great torment, even greater than the way of the cross. God, My Father, gave the dark forces permission to test His Son, which they extensively did. They tortured Me day and night, often I had only one or two hours sleep. In the morning I would lie on My bed, racked with fever ... But the divine power stood by Me; it flowed into My soul and into the physical body ...

The Lord of life led Me to those who became My apostles.
Those men did not go with Me without questions and proof. I worked for some of them as a carpenter. I repaired their houses and barns,

helped where I could, healed and soothed illnesses in their families. I earned money which I left to the families.

I did not ask any disciple to go with Me, until their families were well provided for. Each one went with the Nazarene of his free will, because through My selflessness and My speech, they recognized that I was a just man of the people, with a deep faith through which I could do much according to the will of My Father ... And, with a handshake, the families were promised continual support, even when the men were far away.

We worked for everything that we needed for our own lives and those of the families. We accepted all the work that was offered to us. The Lord, the helmsman of our life, arranged things so, that over and over again, we met trustworthy people, to whom the disciples could give their messages and money to support their families.

And so, the Lord took care of My disciples and their families in a natural way, as He did Me. In this, the Lord showed that even on His Son, He actualized His words, which essentially say: Pray and work, for with the sweat of your brow shall you earn your bread! ...

What I did as Jesus among My own were not miracles, but it was the power of the Spirit, which lives in every person. Jesus was thus a symbol for all of mankind. This power, which was in Me as Jesus, is in every soul and is expressed with the following words: 'You could do even greater things than I have done.' ...

Mankind should live the law of My Father, then everything would be possible for it, too, because the divine law is the genetic makeup of the soul ... I have taught you everything that you need for a divine life. For the coming time I essentially said: 'There will come a time when I will tell you much more, for today you cannot yet understand it.'

For this reason, it is My request as Jesus and, today, the request of the Christ: Do not cling to blind leaders of the blind. When a blind man leads another blind man, both fall into the ditch. The ditch symbolizes the astral spheres where the blind leaders continue to bind their unknowing sheep to themselves, teaching them the same things they taught them in the flesh. They proclaim the word of God to My unknowing children, which does not come from their heart, but from a wrong attitude that they themselves acquired through dogmatic conceptions ....

Jesus, the Christ, also revealed:
"Who was Jesus of Nazareth? A spiritually irradiated person who was one with His Father in heaven. Through the power of the law, I

brought salvation to all souls. What I did for the people as Jesus, was acclaimed as miracles by the world. Those souls, which had gone through only two or three incarnations, did not have to wait for the Redeemer-deed; they could return to the kingdom of light at any time. These souls still had the power of ascension in them. For all others, I again brought and vivified in them the spiritual powers, for everything is contained in all things, also in the souls of the people ...

My children, the Kingdom of Heaven penetrates ever deeper into the hearts of those who look to Me. My words will be fulfilled in all the soul realms. Verily I say to you, whoever does not change himself and become like a little child, trusting and good, will not attain the kingdom of heaven.

The meaning is the following: Whoever clings to his intellectual knowledge, striving only for external riches and affirming the external prestige in his life, will someday have a very difficult time with his ego. Surrender to God as a child and follow His commandments, then God will reveal much to you through Me. Then the person will penetrate into the depths of his soul, where the child slumbers in the Father. The person should awaken the child, so that the spirit body can unfold and be carried higher and higher through the indwelling Christ in you.

The Son of Man has come to vivify all souls. Woe to those who maltreat My just servants in word and deed! It would be better if they had not been born. Because before such souls can attain a rebirth in the Spirit, many eons of time will pass. Therefore, forgive everyone and watch what comes out of your mouth, so that My redemption can be accomplished in you ...

'The Good Shepherd leaves 99 sheep, to find and bring home the one that was lost.' This statement means that no soul will be lost. It also says that God is benevolent, for He breathed His breath into all life. For this reason, He will not destroy any soul.

Never speak of eternal damnation and the punishment of God. God, the Lord, does not damn or punish you. The person carries his own rod in his hand, for what he sows, he will also reap.

The statement about the Good Shepherd points to the All-unity and the love of the Father. In Christ, He goes after every soul – even if it takes eons. God is the timeless and spaceless eternal Spirit that dwells in every soul. He will neither damn nor destroy you, because He lives in you ...

To this very day, mankind has not understood its Redeemer. This is why many people and souls will endure the suffering that I lived through as Jesus. Concerning this, I also gave mankind a symbol for what is to come. The path of suffering is mankind's development, because it does not remember the cross of redemption, but falls ever deeper into sin. Mankind will crucify itself through this. All souls bear redemption within them; this is why no soul will be lost. Man, however, will walk his way of the cross and crucify himself ...

O you deluded people, when will your spiritual body be in the eternal Jerusalem? The Son of Man has brought you freedom, but you keep clinging to those whose depravity I already denounced as Jesus ... Whoever deems himself to be more than My people is a hypocrite; you should not listen to him. So listen only to Christ, who lives in you. Anyone can hear Me if he does the will of My Father. 'Whoever exalts himself will be humbled, and whoever humbles himself will be exalted,' for this is how it is written in your scriptures. Call no one Rabbi, (that is, priest,) *only One is your master, Jesus Christ – you are all brothers.*

Your church authorities today again have prestige before the people. Their earthly works are not done according to the law of God. In the kingdom of My Father, they will be the poorest of the poor, because they were already rewarded by the world ..."

Jesus, the Christ, Himself, revealed as follows regarding the Last Supper:
"The Last Supper with My disciples was also a symbol for mankind. 'Take and eat', He said, ,this is My body,' which means: Through My spiritual resurrection, I Am the light in you, the light which purifies your spiritual body. If you believe in My resurrection and fulfill the commandments of My Father, you will attain re-

birth through Me, for I have come to purify your souls by awakening the spirit.

The meaning of the statement: 'This is My blood, which will be shed for the forgiveness of sins,' is that the blood is the spirit of the soul. It has to be awakened anew, so that the divine elements of the soul – these are the natures of God – align themselves with the divine pull. However, the soul of the one who does not accept My blood – which is the Spirit of truth – will remain unclean until it, the soul, believes in the light of the world and purifies itself through the light, which has begotten itself in every soul through the deed of redemption ...

I also spoke in the following sense:
Woe to those who do not accept My blood and do not act in accordance with the Spirit of God. Through their disbelief, they displace

My blood – the flowing Spirit of God – and create more causes. They will bleed to death in their effects. I have come to redeem the blood of mankind through the Spirit of truth, and to free man from his bad habits and vices. If mankind does not accept its Deliverer, but spurns Him, it will bleed to death. The cause is the disbelief, which will cause their blasphemies to increase, thus becoming effective and cruel ...

My children, each day you should eat your meals with Me. Give thanks for everything that comes from the hands of the Father, for He, the great God, wants only what is good for His children. Everything you receive for your well-being is a divine act of grace, which will strengthen and support you, spiritually, as well as physically. Give thanks in the morning, at noon and at night. Ask for His blessing again and again, then your meals will be blessed each time, and My Spirit will be consciously among you."

In His words of revelation, Jesus, the Christ, also described what happened then, about 2000 years ago:

"Tear-streaked and in prayer, I knelt in the Garden of Gethsemane, wringing My hands and begging for strength for the physical body. 'O My children,' so said the Christ of God, 'if only you could feel the willpower of a soul that wants to only absolutely fulfill the will of the Lord. For not only did Jesus, the man, speak: 'Lord, only Your will be done,' but also the powerful soul and the all-pervading Spirit. This cry of the soul gave Jesus renewed strength, to bear what was to come.

After the cry of My soul, I felt the entire greatness of the Christ of God in Me, the eternally willing, serving Son of His Father. While the soul cried out its affirmation of will to My Father, I felt the perfect and absolute Godhead in Me. It is the perfect connection, which I, in the Christ of God, want to express. It means unity with God and His omnipresence.

After this cry of My soul, My entire soul opened, and I saw much more than during My journey over the Earth. I saw the open heavens and recognized the perfection of God, into which the Christ entered. I saw My spiritual being in all life, especially in all souls – whether incarnate or discarnate. The vision for the great event as a whole was entirely open to Me. The Son of God was at that same moment the Christ of God, which means that God in Christ is the Deliverer and Redeemer of all fallen life."

Through His prophetess, Christ continued to reveal more to us:

"As long as your sun is the cold splendor of the churches and dwellings you have built, in which you worship your idols, you will not enter the Kingdom of God. Only when man and man's soul crucify themselves and surrender all human weaknesses to the cross and become the child of God, will the soul be able to feel the power of the erected cross. With your arrogance and your intellect, with your earthly dignities and titles, as well as with your earthly crown, you will not enter the kingdom of My Father.

Oh see, many who walked on this Earth in honor will live in the spheres of purification and will have to endure similar things from those whom they oppressed and who cannot forgive them for it.

O recognize, the fight came before the victory over the darkness. Every single soul may now fight with Me for the victory of the inner life ... I have gone before you, so that you may follow Me through the power of the Christ of

God in you. Therefore, follow the commandment of commandments! For whatever you do the least of My brothers, you have done to Me. This truth is grounded in you, and through this you can resurrect and go home ...

Be diligent in the Spirit and love the Father above all and your neighbor as yourself. Love the Father's entire Creation ...
I, the Christ of God, Am the key to the gates of heaven. You will find this key by way of the divine attributes of the soul: Order, Will, Wisdom, Earnestness, Patience, Love and Mercy."

In the great revelation of the Christ of God, »*This Is My Word – Alpha and Omega*«, Christ explains the following in the prophetic word:
"The life in God includes not only one's neighbor, but all other forms of life like animals, plants, minerals and stones; for all Being bears the life, God.

The one who is in unity with life neither kills animals nor destroys plants willfully. He also respects the life – the forces of consciousness – of the minerals and stones ... The one who relies on the flesh also consumes flesh. The one who relies on the Spirit nourishes himself with what the Earth gives him, just as it was in former times .... In the course of the generations, blood sacrifices will no longer exist; for people will recognize that they do not honor God with this and that their self-invented gods do not react to their way of thinking and acting. Recognize that the one who no longer envies, who no longer quarrels, who no longer binds and no longer wants to dominate and be the greatest is a man of true peace ... Mankind today lives in a great turn of time from the old sinful world to the New Era."

More words of Christ from the work of revelation, *»This Is My Word«:*

"When this change has been accomplished ... people will fulfill the laws of God more and more and it will be as I foretold as Jesus of Nazareth: There will be one Shepherd and one flock, and the nations will be one people. Then any kind of blood offering will be abolished as well as the eating of animals.

That which is base, satanic, is coming to an end. For more and more people, the life in and with God is turning into a need. Therefore, the Earth, too, will purify itself and nourish the children of God as it was at the beginning of the human race. Mother Earth again gives in abundance to the inhabitants of the Earth what they require for their earthly body. This is then the pure, in turn, for the bodies which are mostly pure.

Recognize, that peace and true Christianity can come into this world only through people who have ennobled their souls with the a-

dornment of virtue and humility, with peaceful thoughts, selfless words and deeds.

I Am the way, the truth and the life. The one who raises his soul to Me also finds his way to Me. And the one who lives in Me, the truth, is free from outer ties and from the trumpery of this world. The one who lives in the truth fills all words and things with life, because he is filled, himself, with the Spirit of God.

To the one who fulfills the law of life, the love, God is manifest in all people, animals, plants, minerals, stones and in all the powers of the All. Nothing remains hidden to the one who opens himself to God. But from the one who wants to hide from God because of his sin, the things and powers of the All are hidden."

Through the prophetic word for our time, Christ gave the following explanations:

"The words of the one who just preaches and teaches the word of God, without having actualized it, do not enter into the heart of his neighbor; they become a boomerang to the one who sends out the word. And so, the one who merely preaches and teaches the word of God, without having actualized it, cannot fill it with strength and power because he is himself without strength.

The person who does not give from the fulfillment of the law, from God, but only spreads what he has read and considers to be the truth, is not a teacher of the truth – whether he is a theologian, priest, pastor or a believer in the Bible, even when he bears a high title ...

Therefore, examine with the eyes of justice, then you will recognize the righteous and the false teachers by their fruits.

The one who lives in the truth perceives what others do not see and hears what others do not hear; and so, he will leave to each his own belief.

Until all souls have again attained the conscious filiation in God, I remain the Redeemer of all souls and people, Christ, the key to the door of life."

Many, very many words of revelation from the Christ of God about His life on Earth, given through the mouth of a prophet are compiled here. For many of you, as for us, it is very special to learn through the prophetic word from the risen Christ of God himself, about His life and teaching as Jesus of Nazareth.

Jesus, the Christ, also said: "My sheep know My voice" – and so, more words are not necessary.

Read also ...

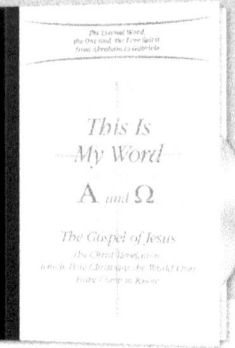

This Is My Word
A & Ω
*The Gospel of Jesus
The Christ Revelation,
Which True Christians
the World Over
Have Come to now*

A book that allows you to get to Jesus, the Christ. The truth about His works und life as Jesus of Nazareth.

From the Table of Contents: The childhood and youth of Jesus • The falsification of the teachings of Jesus of Nazareth during the past 2000 years • Purpose and meaning of life on Earth • Jesus taught the law of sowing and reaping • Prerequisites for healing the body • Jesus teaches about marriage • The Sermon on the Mount • About the nature of God • God does not get angry or punish • The teaching of "eternal damnation" is a mockery of God • Jesus exposes the scribes and Pharisees as hypocrites • Jesus loved the animals and always stood up for them • The one who lives in God is one with all creatures • The human being violates and destroys the life on Earth • The extinction of many species of animals • The law of sowing and reaping also holds true in dealing with creation • Selfless love, the key to understanding and helping one's neighbor and to insight into the causal law and overcoming it • About death, reincarnation and life • Equality of men and women • The true meaning of the Redeemer-deed of Christ ... and much, much more.

With a short autobiography of Gabriele, the prophetess and emissary of God for this time that includes a charcoal drawing of herself.

1194 pp., Soft-Bound, $ 15.00, Order No. S007en.
ISBN: 978-1-890841-38-6

Biography

The Emissary of the Christ of God, His Prophetess of Today, Gabriele

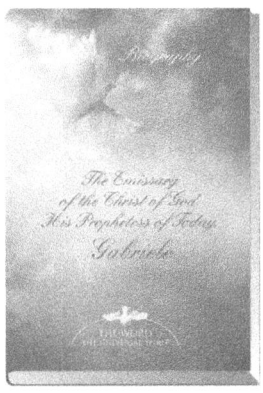

"I still have much to say to you, but you could not bear it now. However, I will send you the Spirit of Truth who will guide you into all truth." Thus spoke Jesus of Nazareth over two thousand years ago.

Gabriele is living proof that, even today, in our time, God will not be silenced. For the free Spirit blows where it will. She is proof that God, the Father of us all, loves His children. For He does not forsake us – not even in a time of disasters and earth upheavals, into which we have maneuvered ourselves.

With an Audio-CD:
"Deep Breathing" and "Abide in You" – 2 Meditations
"You Spurn the One God and Believe in Eternal Damnation. I Am the God of Love" – A God-Father Revelation

316 pp., Softbound, $15.00, Order No. S550en
ISBN: 978-1-890841-73-7

Order a catalog of all books, CDs and DVDs!
THE WORD – THE UNIVERSAL SPIRIT
P.O. Box 3549, Woodbridge, CT 06525
1-800-846-2691 / www.Universal-Spirit.org

www.ingramcontent.com/pod-product-compliance
Lightning Source LLC
Chambersburg PA
CBHW041314110526
44591CB00022B/2914